LIVING IN HIS LIGHT:
Understanding Your
NEW IDENTITY
In Christ

LIVING IN HIS LIGHT:
Understanding Your
NEW IDENTITY
In Christ

By

Nick Imoru

Achievers Publishing
Calgary, Canada

LIVING IN HIS LIGHT: UNDERSTANDING YOUR NEW IDENTITY IN CHRIST
Copyright © 2024 By Nicholas Imoru

ISBN: 978-1-989291-04-7

Published in Canada, by
Achievers Publishing

Canadian Cataloguing in Publication (CIP)
A Record of this Publication is available from the Library and Archives Canada (LAC).

For further information or permission, address:
Achievers Publishing
Calgary, Canada
E-mail: info@achieverspublishing.com
www.achieverspublishing.com

Printed in Canada for Achievers Publishing

Dedication

This book is lovingly dedicated to all new believers in Christ—those who have chosen to accept Jesus as their Lord and Savior. May this journey of discovering your new identity in Him fill you with the light of His love, the strength of His grace, and the joy of His eternal promises. As you walk in the fullness of His truth, may you be transformed into the glorious reflection of His light.

Table of Contents

INTRODUCTION

Overview of the New Life in Christ

When you accept Jesus Christ as your Lord and Savior, you enter into a new, transformed life—what the Bible calls being "born again." This new life in Christ is not merely a change of behavior or developing a set of new habits; it is a complete transformation of your inner being. As a believer, you are now a new creation, reborn and renewed in your spirit, which changes your identity, purpose, and relationship with God.

The new life in Christ means you are no longer defined by your past, your sins, or your failures. Instead, you are defined by your relationship with Christ. You are forgiven, redeemed, and empowered by the Holy Spirit to live a victorious life that reflects God's glory. This book will guide you through understanding what it truly means to live in this new identity. It will explore the fundamental truths of who you are in Christ, what has been accomplished on your behalf, and how you can walk in the fullness of this new life.

As you embark on this journey, you will discover the richness of your inheritance in Christ, the power available to you as a child of God, and the unshakeable love that God has for you. This is not just knowledge for the mind; it is a transformative truth meant to revolutionize every aspect of your life. Embrace your new identity and allow the truths in this book to deepen your relationship with Christ and empower you to live a life that is pleasing to God.

Purpose and Aim of the Book

The purpose of this book is to help you understand and embrace your new identity in Christ. Many believers struggle to fully grasp what it means to be born again and often live below the privileges that are theirs as children of God. This book aims to bridge that gap by providing clear, biblical insights into your new life in Christ, making it practical and applicable to everyday living.

The aim of this book is not just to inform but to transform. As you read each chapter, you will be guided through key aspects of your identity in Christ—who you are, what you have, and what you can do now that you are in Christ. You will learn about the righteousness, justification, sanctification, and deliverance that are yours through Jesus. You will understand the power of the Holy Spirit living within you and how to navigate the challenges and temptations that come your way.

Ultimately, this book is designed to equip you with the knowledge and confidence to live boldly as a new creation. By the end of this book, you should have a clearer understanding of your position in Christ, the benefits of your salvation, and the practical steps you can take to live out your faith. It is our prayer that this book will be a tool that helps you grow in your walk with God and encourages you to live a life that is fully aligned with His will.

How to Use This Book

This book is structured to be a comprehensive guide to understanding your new life in Christ. To get the most out of it, it is recommended that you read it chapter by chapter, taking time to reflect on each section. Here are a few suggestions on how to use this book effectively:

1. **Read Prayerfully**: Begin each reading session with a prayer, asking the Holy Spirit to open your eyes to the truths in God's Word. The insights in this book are grounded in Scripture, and it is the Holy Spirit who will make them come alive to you.

2. **Reflect and Meditate**: Take time to reflect on the verses and truths presented in each chapter. Meditate on how they apply to your life. It might be helpful to keep a journal to jot down your thoughts, revelations, and any questions that arise.

3. **Apply What You Learn**: This book is not just for reading but for application. As you go through each chapter, look for ways to apply the principles to your daily life. Whether it's embracing your righteousness, walking in your deliverance, or relying on the Holy Spirit, put the teachings into practice.

4. **Study the Scriptures**: Throughout the book, you will find numerous scriptural references. Take the time to look them up, study them in their context, and let the Word of God speak directly to you.

5. **Share and Discuss**: Consider discussing what you're learning with other believers. Sharing your insights and hearing others' perspectives can enrich your understanding and strengthen your faith. This book can also be used in group studies or discipleship settings.

6. **Revisit and Review**: Understanding your new life in Christ is a journey, and it's okay to revisit chapters as needed. If there's a particular truth or concept that resonates with you, return to it, and let it sink deeper into your heart.

This book is more than just information; it's an invitation to a deeper, more fulfilling walk with Christ. May it be a blessing to you as you journey into the fullness of your new life in Him.

CHAPTER 1: WHO YOU REALLY ARE

1. Understanding Your True Self

The Spirit, Soul, and Body

To fully grasp your new life in Christ, it's crucial to understand who you really are. Many people identify themselves primarily by their physical appearance or their achievements, but these are not the core of your identity. The Bible teaches that man is a triune being, composed of spirit, soul, and body (1 Thessalonians 5:23).

Your body is what you see in the mirror; it's your physical form, which interacts with the physical world through your five senses—sight, hearing, touch, taste, and smell. However, your body is not the real you; it's merely the outer shell that houses your true self.

Your soul is your mind, will, and emotions. It's where your thoughts, decisions, and feelings reside. The soul is important because it processes information from both the physical and spiritual realms, influencing how you live your life.

But the most significant part of you is your spirit. Your spirit is the real you—the innermost part of your being. It is the part of you that connects with God, as God is a Spirit (John 4:24). When you are born again, it is your spirit that is renewed and made alive in Christ. This renewed spirit is the foundation of your new identity.

The Real You: The Human Spirit

Your human spirit is the essence of who you are. Before being born again, your spirit was separated from God due to sin. However, when you accepted Christ, your spirit was reborn, reconnecting you with God and aligning you with His purpose. The Bible refers to this inner man as the *"hidden man of the heart"* (1 Peter 3:4). It's this hidden, imperishable part of you that is of great worth in God's sight. Understanding that you are fundamentally a spirit being changes how you see yourself and how you live your life.

2. The Essence of the Inner Man

The Hidden Man of the Heart

The Apostle Peter describes the real you as the *"hidden man of the heart,"* (1 Peter 3:4) which is incorruptible and valuable in God's sight. This hidden man is your spirit, and it is adorned with qualities that are precious to God, such as a meek and quiet spirit. This verse highlights the importance of nurturing your spirit, as it is the core of your identity and the part of you that interacts with God on a personal level.

Biblical Illustrations: Lazarus and the Rich Man

To further illustrate the reality of the human spirit, let's consider the story of Lazarus and the rich man as told by Jesus in Luke 16:19-31. In this parable, both Lazarus and the rich man died, and although their bodies were buried, their spirits continued to exist in different realms—Lazarus in Abraham's bosom and the rich man in torment.

This story emphasizes that even after physical death, the spirit remains conscious and retains its identity and senses. The rich man, though dead, could see, feel, remember, and communicate, proving that the spirit carries all the consciousness of a person beyond physical life. This understanding reveals that your spirit is the true you, and it continues to live on, whether in the presence of God or separated from Him.

3. Created in God's Image

Man as a Spirit Being

From the beginning, God's intent for man was clear: to create a being in His own image and likeness. Genesis 1:26-27 states, "*Then God said, 'Let Us make man in Our image, according to Our likeness...' So God created man in His own image; in the image of God He created him; male and female He created them.*" Since God is Spirit (John 4:24), being made in His image means that you, too, are a spirit being.

God's design for mankind was to have dominion over the earth, but to function in the physical realm, He clothed the spirit man with a body. This body allows you to interact with the material world, but it does not define your essence. Your true nature as a spirit being made in the likeness of God means that you are not limited by your physical form.

The Physical Body as a Vessel

Genesis 2:7 provides further insight: "*And the Lord God formed man of the dust of the ground, and breathed into his nostrils the breath of life; and man became a living soul.*" This verse illustrates how God formed the human body from the dust but gave life through His breath, which represents the spirit. The physical body, therefore, is a vessel—a temporary house for your spirit that enables you to operate in the world.

Understanding that your body is a vessel helps you prioritize your spirit over your physical appearance and limitations. It shifts your focus from the temporary to the eternal, emphasizing the importance of cultivating your spiritual life.

4. Implications of Understanding Your True Self

Living Beyond the Physical

Realizing that you are fundamentally a spirit being changes your perspective on life. You are no longer confined to your physical body or defined by it. This understanding empowers you to live beyond the limitations of the physical world, such as sickness, fear, and lack, because your spirit is connected to God's unlimited power and resources.

Living beyond the physical also means that your priorities shift. You begin to value spiritual growth and development over material gain. Your decisions are guided by your identity in Christ rather than by societal pressures or physical desires. This perspective enables you to live a victorious life, rooted in the reality of who you truly are—a spirit being made in the image of God, with access to His divine nature and power.

Spiritual Realities and Earthly Dominion

Understanding your true self also affects how you exercise dominion on earth. God's original intention was for man to rule over the earth as His representative. As a spirit being, you have authority over the spiritual and physical realms through Christ. This dominion is exercised not through physical strength but through spiritual authority, which comes from your connection with God.

In Christ, you have been given the keys to the Kingdom of Heaven (Matthew 16:19), empowering you to bind and loose, to declare and decree God's will on earth.

By aligning your spirit with God's Word and His purposes, you can navigate life's challenges with confidence, knowing that you have been equipped to reign in life through the power of Christ in you.

CHAPTER 2: YOU ARE NOW A NEW YOU

1. The Moment of Transformation

Born Again: A New Creature

The journey of the new life in Christ begins the moment you are born again. This transformation is not just a symbolic act; it's a profound change that takes place in your spirit. 2 Corinthians 5:17 declares, *"Therefore if any man be in Christ, he is a new creature: old things are passed away; behold, all things are become new."* This verse encapsulates the essence of your transformation in Christ—you have become a new creation.

Being born again means that the old you, with its sinful nature and past mistakes, has been crucified with Christ. The new you is a fresh, untouched creation, unblemished by the past. You are not merely a better version of your old self; you are a completely new being in God's eyes. The former things—old habits, old ways of thinking, and old lifestyles—are gone. In their place is a new life filled with God's righteousness, peace, and joy.

What Happens When You Accept Christ

When you accept Jesus Christ as your Lord and Savior, a supernatural event takes place. Your spirit, which was previously dead in sin, is reborn. This is the essence of the new birth—your spirit is regenerated by the power of the Holy Spirit. In this new state, you are no longer separated from God; instead, you are now united with Him in a personal relationship.

The transformation is instantaneous but also initiates a lifelong journey of growth and sanctification. The Holy Spirit begins to dwell within you, guiding you into all truth and helping you to live according to God's will. This inner change is reflected in your actions, thoughts, and attitudes, gradually shaping you to be more like Christ. It's important to remember that this transformation is not achieved by human effort but is a work of God's grace through faith in Jesus Christ.

2. A Brand-New Creation

Not Refurbished or Reformed but Brand New

It's crucial to understand that when the Bible says you are a new creation, it doesn't mean you are a refurbished or reformed version of your old self. The transformation is not about self-improvement or becoming a better person by human standards. Instead, it is a complete renewal that only God can accomplish.

Think of it like this: when a manufacturer produces a new product, it is brand new, not a recycled or improved version of an old model. Similarly, when God makes you a new creation, He does not simply clean up your past; He creates something entirely new that never existed before. Your new nature is born of God, carrying His divine DNA. This new creation is not bound by your past failures, sins, or the limitations of your old self.

This is a profound truth that sets you free from the mindset of striving to earn God's approval. You are already approved in Christ, not because of what you have done but because of what Christ has done on your behalf. Embrace the fact that you are brand new and let go of the past because it no longer defines you.

Understanding Your New Identity

As a new creation, your identity is now rooted in Christ. This means that your worth, purpose, and destiny are defined by who Christ is and what He has done for you, not by your past or what others think of you. Understanding this new identity is crucial because it influences how you see yourself and how you live your life.

Your new identity includes being righteous, justified, sanctified, and delivered, as you will explore in the coming chapters. You are a child of God, a citizen of Heaven, and a partaker of God's divine nature. This new identity gives you access to the promises of God and the authority to live victoriously. Knowing who you are in Christ is the foundation for living out your new life with confidence and purpose.

3. Living as the New You

Changes in Values and Mindset

The new life in Christ brings with it a new set of values and a transformed mindset. As a new creation, your values are no longer shaped by the world but by the Word of God. What once mattered to you—such as worldly success, approval from others, or material possessions—now takes a backseat to your pursuit of God's kingdom and righteousness.

Romans 12:2 exhorts believers to *"be transformed by the renewing of your mind."* This renewal process involves replacing old, worldly thoughts with God's thoughts, aligning your mindset with your new identity in Christ. It's an ongoing process that requires daily engagement with Scriptures, prayer, and fellowship with other believers.

Your new values reflect the character of Christ: love, humility, patience, kindness, and integrity. As you grow in your understanding of God's Word, you will find that your desires change, and what once seemed important may no longer hold the same appeal. This transformation is evidence of your new life and a testament to the work of the Holy Spirit within you.

Outward Appearance vs. Inner Transformation

While your outward appearance may remain the same, the real change occurs on the inside. It's important not to judge your transformation by external factors, such as how you look or the immediate changes in your circumstances. The true evidence of your new life in Christ is the transformation of your heart and mind.

This inner transformation is reflected in your behavior, attitudes, and the choices you make. As you continue to grow in your relationship with God, the changes on the inside will begin to manifest outwardly. People may notice a difference in how you speak, how you treat others, and how you handle challenges. This is the fruit of the Spirit at work in your life, demonstrating the reality of your new creation.

Living as the new you means embracing the inner transformation that Christ has accomplished and allowing it to influence every aspect of your life. It's a journey of becoming more like Jesus, not through your own strength, but through the power of the Holy Spirit who lives in you. As you yield to His leading, you will find that living as the new you becomes more natural, and the old ways lose their grip on you.

CHAPTER 3: A PARTAKER OF GOD'S NATURE

1. Receiving the Nature of God

Power to Become Children of God

One of the most profound truths of your new life in Christ is that you have received the very nature of God. John 1:12-13 declares, *"But as many as received Him, to them He gave the power to become the sons of God, even to them that believe on His name: which were born, not of blood, nor of the will of the flesh, nor of the will of man, but of God."* This scripture highlights the transformative power of believing in Christ. By receiving Him, you have been given the right and authority to be called a child of God.

This new identity as a child of God is not based on human descent, personal effort, or religious practices; it is a result of being born of God. This spiritual birth imparts to you God's divine nature, making you a part of His family. You are no longer a mere creation of God; you are now His child, with all the rights, privileges, and responsibilities that come with being a member of His household. This new nature empowers you to live a life that reflects God's character and fulfills His purposes for you.

The God-Kind of Life: Eternal Life

As a partaker of God's nature, you have also received eternal life. Eternal life is not just living forever; it is the God-kind of life—life as God has it. 1 John 5:11-13 states, "*And this is the record, that God hath given to us eternal life, and this life is in His Son. He that hath the Son hath life; and he that hath not the Son of God hath not life.*" This life is a gift from God, and it is contained in His Son, Jesus Christ. When you received Christ, you received this eternal life.

This life transcends physical existence; it is a quality of life characterized by righteousness, peace, joy, and power in the Holy Spirit. It is the same life that made it impossible for death to hold Jesus in the grave. Now that this life is in you, it empowers you to live victoriously over sin, sickness, and every challenge that comes your way. Eternal life is the assurance of God's presence within you, guiding, protecting, and sustaining you through all of life's circumstances.

2. The Implications of God's Nature

God's Responsibility Towards You

As a child of God and a partaker of His nature, God takes responsibility for your well-being. Philippians 4:19 reassures you of this truth: *"But my God shall supply all your need according to His riches in glory by Christ Jesus."* This promise highlights that God's provision for you is not based on your ability or resources but on His abundant riches in glory. He knows your needs even before you ask, and He is committed to providing for you as a loving Father.

God's responsibility towards you goes beyond just meeting your physical needs; it encompasses every aspect of your life—spiritual, emotional, mental, and relational. He is your Shepherd who guides you, your Provider who meets your needs, your Healer who restores you, and your Protector who keeps you safe. As His child, you can trust that He is always working for your good, even in difficult times. This assurance allows you to rest in His care, knowing that you are not alone, and that God is actively involved in every detail of your life.

Citizenship in Heaven and the Household of God

Being a partaker of God's nature also means that you have a new citizenship. Philippians 3:20 states, *"For our citizenship is in heaven, from which we also eagerly wait for the Savior, the Lord Jesus Christ."* Your primary identity is now as a citizen of Heaven. This means that your values, priorities, and way of life are no longer dictated by the world but by the principles of God's Kingdom.

As a member of God's household, you have access to the privileges and benefits of being part of His family. You are not an outsider or a guest; you belong to the very household of God, with Jesus Christ as your elder brother. This citizenship grants you access to God's throne of grace, where you can boldly approach Him with your prayers and petitions. It also connects you with a global family of believers, united by the same Spirit and the same divine nature.

Your heavenly citizenship should influence how you live on earth. It calls you to live as an ambassador of Christ, representing His Kingdom in all you do. It also assures you that, no matter what happens in this world, your ultimate home and inheritance are secure in Heaven. This perspective gives you hope, courage, and the strength to persevere through life's challenges, knowing that your true reward is eternal.

3. Living Above Defeat

Resurrection Life: Victory Over Challenges

The God-kind of life that you have received is a resurrection life—one that triumphs over death, sin, and all forms of defeat. Romans 8:11 declares, *"But if the Spirit of Him that raised up Jesus from the dead dwell in you, He that raised up Christ from the dead shall also quicken your mortal bodies by His Spirit that dwelleth in you."* This verse emphasizes that the same power that raised Jesus from the dead now lives in you, energizing and empowering you to overcome every obstacle.

Living above defeat means that you are no longer a victim of circumstances. The resurrection life within you equips you to rise above every challenge, whether it be fear, sickness, financial lack, or any other adversity. This does not mean that you will never face difficulties, but it does mean that you have the power to overcome them through Christ. You are more than a conqueror through Him who loves you (Romans 8:37).

To live in the fullness of this victory, it's essential to continually renew your mind with God's Word, aligning your thoughts with the truth of your new nature. The enemy will try to deceive you into thinking that you are still bound by your old limitations, but the truth is that you have been set free. As you grow in your understanding of who you are in Christ and the power that resides in you, you will find that living above defeat becomes your new normal.

Victory in Christ is not just a one-time event; it is a lifestyle. It's about walking in the awareness of God's presence and power in your life, trusting that He who began a good work in you will carry it on to completion. As you rely on the Holy Spirit, you will experience the abundant life that Jesus promised—a life that is full of peace, joy, purpose, and victory.

CHAPTER 4: YOU ARE THE RIGHTEOUSNESS OF GOD

1. Understanding Righteousness

Nature-Transplant: From Sin to Righteousness

One of the most remarkable aspects of your new identity in Christ is the gift of righteousness. Righteousness is not just a concept; it is a state of being that reflects your new nature in Christ. 2 Corinthians 5:21 states, *"For he hath made him to be sin for us, who knew no sin; that we might be made the righteousness of God in him."* This verse highlights a divine exchange that took place on the cross—Jesus, who was without sin, took on our sin so that we could take on His righteousness.

This "nature-transplant" means that you are no longer defined by your past sins or shortcomings. Through Christ, you have been made righteous, which means you are in right standing with God. This righteousness is not something you earn through good deeds or moral living; it is a gift from God, received through faith in Jesus Christ. It is a new nature that has been imparted to your spirit, enabling you to stand before God without any sense of guilt, condemnation, or fear.

The implications of these are profound. You are no longer under the power of sin because your old sinful nature was nailed to the cross with Christ. Now, you are clothed in His righteousness, and God sees you through the lens of His Son's perfect sacrifice. This truth liberates you from the need to strive for approval or acceptance, as you are already fully accepted and beloved in Christ.

Standing Before God Without Guilt or Fear

As the righteousness of God, you have the incredible privilege of approaching God with confidence. Hebrews 10:19 declares, *"Having therefore, brethren, boldness to enter into the holiest by the blood of Jesus."* This boldness comes from knowing that your sins have been forgiven, and you are covered by the righteousness of Christ. You no longer need to approach God timidly or with a sense of unworthiness;

you can come boldly to His throne of grace, knowing that you are His righteous child.

Romans 5:1 further emphasizes this point: *"Therefore being justified by faith, we have peace with God through our Lord Jesus Christ."* Justification by faith means that you have been declared righteous in God's sight, not because of what you have done, but because of what Jesus has done. This justification brings peace—a peace that comes from knowing that there is no longer a barrier between you and God. You are no longer an enemy of God; you are His beloved child, and nothing can separate you from His love.

Standing before God without guilt or fear transforms your relationship with Him. You can approach Him freely, worship Him fully, and serve Him joyfully, without the burden of trying to earn His favor. This freedom allows you to enjoy your relationship with God, knowing that you are always welcomed in His presence.

2. Living as the Righteousness of God

Practical Implications for Daily Living

Understanding that you are the righteousness of God should influence every aspect of your daily life. Righteousness is not just a theological concept; it is a practical reality that should shape how you think, speak, and act. As the righteousness of God, you are called to live in a way that reflects your new nature. This means making choices that align with God's Word and His standards.

Living as the righteousness of God involves walking in integrity, honesty, and love. It means treating others with kindness and respect, being a person of your word, and living in a way that honors God. Your actions should be a reflection of the righteous nature within you. This doesn't mean you will never make mistakes, but it does mean that when you do, you can quickly repent and return to the path of righteousness because your identity is secure in Christ.

Righteousness also empowers you to overcome sin and temptation. Knowing who you are in Christ gives you the strength to say no to sin and yes to God's will. You are no longer a slave to sin; you are a servant of righteousness. This understanding transforms how you respond to challenges and temptations, equipping you to live victoriously in every situation.

Embracing a Guilt-Free Life in Christ

One of the greatest benefits of being the righteousness of God is the freedom from guilt and condemnation. Romans 8:1 assures us, *"There is therefore now no condemnation to them which are in Christ Jesus."* Guilt and condemnation are tools that the enemy uses to keep you trapped in your past mistakes and to undermine your confidence in God's love and forgiveness. But as a righteous child of God, you have been set free from the weight of guilt.

Embracing a guilt-free life means letting go of the past and refusing to allow mistakes or failures to define you. It means choosing to believe what God says about you rather than the lies of the enemy. When guilt tries to creep in, you can stand on the truth of God's Word that you are forgiven, cleansed, and made righteous by the blood of Jesus.

Living guilt-free also means extending grace to yourself and others. Just as God has forgiven you, you are called to forgive others and to live in the freedom of that forgiveness. This mindset allows you to experience the fullness of God's joy and peace, unencumbered by the burdens of the past. It empowers you to move forward with confidence, knowing that your righteousness in Christ is unshakable and eternal.

CHAPTER 5: YOU ARE JUSTIFIED

1. The Meaning of Justification

Declared Not Guilty

Justification is a legal term that means to be declared righteous or not guilty. In the context of your new life in Christ, justification signifies that God has declared you righteous, removing all charges of guilt against you because of your faith in Jesus Christ. Romans 5:1 states, *"Therefore being justified by faith, we have peace with God through our Lord Jesus Christ."* This verse captures the essence of justification: it is by faith, not by works, that you are justified, and this justification brings you into a state of peace with God.

Being justified means that all accusations against you have been dismissed. God, the righteous Judge, has examined your case, and because of the sacrifice of Jesus, He has rendered the verdict of "not guilty." This declaration is not based on your righteousness but on

Christ's perfect righteousness, which has been credited to your account. When God looks at you, He sees you through the lens of Christ's righteousness, making you blameless in His sight.

This truth is liberating because it means that your standing with God is secure, not because of what you have done but because of what Christ has done. You are justified by grace through faith, and this justification is a gift that you receive, not something you earn. It is a foundational truth of the Gospel that assures you of your acceptance before God.

Christ's Sacrifice and Your Justification

The basis of your justification is the sacrificial death of Jesus Christ. 1 Peter 2:22 says, *"Who did no sin, neither was guile found in His mouth."* Jesus lived a sinless life, and yet He chose to take on the punishment for your sins so that you could be justified. His sacrifice on the cross was the ultimate payment for sin, satisfying the demands of God's justice.

Jesus' death and resurrection made it possible for you to be justified because He took your place, bearing the penalty that you deserved. His righteousness was exchanged for your sinfulness in what is often referred to as the Great Exchange. He took your guilt, shame, and punishment, and in return, He gave you His righteousness, honor, and peace.

This divine exchange is the heart of justification. It means that you no longer have to carry the weight of your sins because Jesus has already paid the price. His perfect obedience and sacrifice have secured your justification, and now you stand before God as if you had never sinned. This is not a temporary or conditional status; it is a permanent declaration by God that you are justified forever in Christ.

2. The Benefits of Justification

Peace with God

One of the immediate benefits of justification is peace with God. This peace is not merely a feeling but a state of being that results from being reconciled to God. Romans 5:1 emphasizes that through justification, you have peace with God. This peace signifies the end of hostility between you and God. Before justification, sin created a barrier between you and God, resulting in separation and conflict. However, through Christ's sacrifice, the barrier has been removed, and you are now at peace with your Creator.

Peace with God brings a profound sense of security and assurance. You no longer have to fear God's wrath or judgment because your sins have been forgiven, and you have been justified. This peace also provides stability in your relationship with God, allowing you to approach Him with confidence and boldness. It is a peace that transcends circumstances, knowing that you are firmly established in God's favor and love.

Moreover, peace with God extends to every area of your life. It affects how you interact with others, how you handle challenges, and how you view the world around you. This peace is a stabilizing force that anchors your soul in the midst of life's storms. It is a constant reminder that, regardless of what happens, you are in right standing with God, and nothing can change that.

Living Without Condemnation

Another significant benefit of justification is the freedom from condemnation. 2 Corinthians 5:19 says, *"To wit, that God was in Christ, reconciling the world unto himself, not imputing their trespasses unto them;*

and hath committed unto us the word of reconciliation." This verse underscores that because of Christ's work, God no longer counts your sins against you. You have been reconciled to God, and there is no condemnation for those who are in Christ Jesus (Romans 8:1).

Living without condemnation means that you are free from the guilt and shame that sin brings. It means that you do not have to live under the weight of past mistakes or fear future judgment. Justification assures you that your sins have been dealt with once and for all, and you are no longer subject to condemnation. This freedom empowers you to live boldly and confidently in your identity as a justified child of God.

The enemy often tries to bring condemnation by reminding you of your failures and shortcomings. However, as someone who is justified, you can stand firm in the truth that you are forgiven and cleansed by the blood of Jesus. You do not have to accept the enemy's accusations because God has already declared you not guilty. This freedom from condemnation allows you to walk in the fullness of God's grace, embracing the abundant life that Christ has provided.

Living without condemnation also means extending grace to others. Just as you have been forgiven, you are called to forgive those who wrong you. This cycle of receiving and extending grace creates a culture of mercy and love that reflects God's heart. It allows you to build relationships that are not based on judgment or criticism but on the same grace that has justified you.

CHAPTER 6: YOU ARE SANCTIFIED

1. Understanding Sanctification

Set Apart: From the World to God

Sanctification is a vital aspect of your new identity in Christ. To be sanctified means to be set apart, dedicated to God, and made holy. It is the process by which God separates you from the world and its influences, aligning you with His purposes and making you fit for His service. 1 Corinthians 6:11 states, *"And such were some of you: but ye are washed, but ye are sanctified, but ye are justified in the name of the Lord Jesus, and by the Spirit of our God."* This verse emphasizes that sanctification is part of the transformative work that God has done in you through Christ.

When you became born again, God sanctified you, setting you apart from the world and consecrating you to Himself. This initial sanctification is an act of God's grace, declaring you holy and belonging to Him. You are no longer defined by your past or the world's standards; you are now identified by your relationship with God and His righteousness in you. This separation from the world is not about physical withdrawal but about a change in your heart and values. You are in the world, but you are not of it; your life is now governed by God's Kingdom principles.

Sanctification signifies that you have been cleansed, purified, and dedicated to God's service. It is a mark of your new identity, showing that you belong to God and are under His authority. Understanding this helps you live with a sense of purpose and destiny, knowing that your life is set apart for God's glory.

The Two Phases of Sanctification

Sanctification involves two main phases: positional sanctification and progressive sanctification.

- **Positional Sanctification:** This occurs the moment you accept Christ as your Savior. In this phase, God declares you sanctified, meaning you are set apart for His purposes from the very beginning of your Christian journey. It's a one-time event that reflects your new standing in Christ. Positional sanctification is the foundation of your relationship with God, establishing you as His own and freeing you from the penalty of sin.

- **Progressive Sanctification:** This phase is an ongoing process where God continues to work in your life, shaping and molding you to become more like Christ. It is the daily transformation that takes place as you grow in your faith, learn God's Word, and apply it to your life. Progressive sanctification involves the Holy Spirit's continual work of refining your character, purifying your motives, and guiding you into all truth. It is a lifelong journey of becoming more holy, more Christlike, and more aligned with God's will.

Progressive sanctification requires your active participation. While God provides the power and guidance, you must choose to cooperate with the Holy Spirit, yielding to His leading and obeying His Word. This phase involves daily decisions to turn away from sin, reject worldly influences, and pursue God's ways. It is a process of growing in grace and learning to walk in the Spirit, allowing God's sanctifying work to take deeper root in your life.

2. The Process of Renewing Your Mind

Transformation Through God's Word

A critical aspect of sanctification is the renewal of your mind. Romans 12:2 instructs, "*And be not conformed to this world: but be ye transformed by the renewing of your mind, that ye may prove what is that good, and acceptable, and perfect, will of God.*" This verse highlights the importance of not conforming to the world's patterns but instead being transformed by the continual renewal of your mind.

The renewal of your mind involves changing the way you think, moving away from worldly perspectives and adopting a mindset that aligns with God's truth. It is through God's Word that your mind is renewed. As you study, meditate on, and apply the Scriptures, your thoughts, beliefs, and attitudes are reshaped according to God's standards. The Word of God is powerful and transformative; it has the ability to cleanse, correct, and guide you into God's perfect will.

Renewing your mind is not a one-time event but an ongoing process. Every day, you are bombarded with messages and influences from the world that can lead you away from God's truth. Therefore, it is essential to consistently immerse yourself in God's Word, allowing it to wash over your mind and keep your focus on Him. This daily practice of engaging with Scripture helps you stay rooted in your identity in Christ and empowers you to live a sanctified life.

The transformation that comes from renewing your mind leads to a life that is pleasing to God. As your mind is renewed, your actions will follow, reflecting the righteousness and holiness that God has called you to. This process not only changes how you think but also how you live, enabling you to fulfill God's purposes for your life.

Continuous Renewal and Growth

Sanctification is a journey of continuous renewal and growth. It is not about perfection but about progression—growing in your faith and becoming more like Christ each day. Philippians 1:6 assures you that *"He which hath begun a good work in you will perform it until the day of Jesus Christ."* This promise reminds you that God is committed to your sanctification, and He will faithfully continue the work He has started in you.

Continuous renewal means that you are always learning, always growing, and always being transformed by God's Spirit. It involves regular self-examination, repentance, and a willingness to let go of anything that hinders your walk with God. It's about staying humble, teachable, and open to the Holy Spirit's correction and guidance.

Growth in sanctification also comes through trials and challenges. God often uses difficult circumstances to refine your character and draw you closer to Him. These experiences teach you to rely on God's strength, develop perseverance, and deepen your faith. While the process may not always be easy, it is through these times of testing that you experience significant spiritual growth.

Your role in continuous renewal is to remain steadfast in your commitment to God, to seek His presence daily, and to cultivate a lifestyle of worship, prayer, and obedience. As you do, you will find that God's sanctifying power will continue to shape you, making you more like Christ and enabling you to live a life that glorifies Him.

CHAPTER 7: YOU ARE DELIVERED

1. Deliverance from Darkness

Transferred to God's Kingdom

Deliverance is a fundamental aspect of your new life in Christ. It signifies that you have been rescued from the power of darkness and brought into the glorious light of God's Kingdom. Colossians 1:12-13 beautifully captures this transformation: *"Giving thanks unto the Father, which hath made us meet to be partakers of the inheritance of the saints in light: who hath delivered us from the power of darkness, and hath translated us into the kingdom of his dear Son."* This passage highlights that deliverance is not just a change in location but a complete shift in spiritual authority and allegiance.

Before accepting Christ, you were under the dominion of darkness, subjected to the influences and powers of sin, fear, and spiritual bondage. However, through Christ's redemptive work, you have been transferred from this realm of darkness into God's Kingdom. This is a kingdom of light, love, and truth, where Jesus reigns as King and you are a valued citizen. Your deliverance is a spiritual repositioning that alters your destiny and your identity, freeing you from the grip of the enemy.

Being delivered from darkness means that you no longer belong to the kingdom of Satan. You are now a part of God's family, and His light dispels the darkness that once controlled your life. This new position grants you access to the inheritance of the saints, which includes God's promises, His protection, and His divine favor. It also means that you are no longer bound by the limitations of your past or the lies of the enemy. You are free to live in the fullness of God's Kingdom, where His power and authority are at work in and through you.

Freedom from Past Bondages

Deliverance also means freedom from the bondages of your past. Whether it's the chains of sin, destructive habits, generational curses, or spiritual oppression,

Christ's deliverance sets you free from anything that held you captive. In John 8:36, Jesus declares, *"If the Son therefore shall make you free, ye shall be free indeed."* This freedom is not partial or temporary; it is a complete and lasting liberation that transforms every aspect of your life.

The power of Christ's deliverance extends to every area where darkness once reigned. It breaks the chains of addiction, heals emotional wounds, and releases you from the oppressive thoughts and behaviors that once dominated your life. You are no longer defined by your past failures, sins, or struggles. In Christ, you have a new identity as a redeemed and delivered child of God.

Embracing this deliverance means letting go of old mindsets and behaviors that no longer align with your new identity. It involves rejecting the lies of the enemy that try to pull you back into bondage and standing firm in the truth of God's Word. You are no longer a slave to fear, sin, or any form of spiritual bondage. Christ's deliverance empowers you to walk in freedom, confident in your new position as a citizen of God's Kingdom.

2. Living in the Light of Deliverance

Confidence in God's Protection

As someone who has been delivered, you can live with the assurance of God's constant protection. Psalm 23:1 declares, *"The Lord is my shepherd; I shall not want."* This verse encapsulates the confidence that comes from knowing that God is your protector, provider, and guide. Just as a shepherd cares for and defends his sheep, God watches over you with unwavering attention and care.

Living in the light of deliverance means that you do not have to fear the threats or attacks of the enemy. God's deliverance includes His ongoing protection, ensuring that you are safe from spiritual harm. The Lord surrounds you with His presence, His angels, and His promises, creating a hedge of protection around your life. This protection is not passive but active, as God continually works on your behalf to keep you from falling into the traps and schemes of the enemy.

Your confidence in God's protection allows you to live boldly and fearlessly, knowing that no weapon formed against you shall prosper (Isaiah 54:17). This assurance gives you peace in the midst of life's storms, courage in the face of challenges, and strength when confronted with opposition. You can rest in the fact that God is your shield, your fortress, and your deliverer, who fights for you and ensures your victory.

Embracing Freedom in Christ

Living in the light of deliverance also means fully embracing the freedom that Christ has given you. John 8:36 declares, *"If the Son therefore shall make you free, ye shall be free indeed."* This freedom is not just about being free from sin but encompasses every area of your life—freedom in your thoughts, your emotions, your decisions, and your actions.

Embracing this freedom involves walking in the authority that Christ has given you. You have the power to reject the lies of the enemy and to live according to God's truth. You no longer have to be bound by fear, anxiety, or any form of spiritual oppression. Instead, you can live with joy, peace, and confidence, knowing that Christ's deliverance has set you free from every chain.

Living in freedom also means exercising your authority in Christ. You have been given the power to bind and loose, to declare God's promises over your life, and to stand firm against the forces of darkness. This authority is not based on your strength but on Christ's victory on the cross. As you embrace this freedom, you can step into your God-given purpose and live a life that glorifies Him.

To fully embrace your freedom in Christ, it's important to renew your mind with God's Word, to surround yourself with a community of believers who can support and encourage you, and to remain steadfast in your commitment to follow Christ. Freedom is both a gift and a responsibility, calling you to live in a way that reflects the deliverance you have received. As you do, you will experience the fullness of life that Jesus promised—a life marked by freedom, purpose, and victory.

CHAPTER 8: GOD'S SPIRIT ABIDES IN YOU

1. The Indwelling of the Holy Spirit

Receiving the Holy Spirit at New Birth

One of the greatest blessings of your new life in Christ is the indwelling of the Holy Spirit. At the moment of your new birth, when you accepted Jesus Christ as your Lord and Savior, the Holy Spirit came to dwell within you. This indwelling is a powerful testimony to your new identity as a child of God. It marks the beginning of a dynamic relationship where God's Spirit lives in you, guiding, teaching, and empowering you.

Receiving the Holy Spirit is not a separate experience from salvation; it is an integral part of it. Romans 8:9 affirms, *"But ye are not in the flesh, but in the Spirit, if so be that the Spirit of God dwell in you. Now if any man have not the Spirit of Christ, he is none of his."* This means that every believer has the Holy Spirit living within them. His presence is the evidence of your salvation and the guarantee of your inheritance in Christ (Ephesians 1:13-14).

The Holy Spirit's indwelling transforms you from the inside out. He regenerates your spirit, making you alive to God and enabling you to live according to God's will. The Spirit empowers you to overcome sin, to grow in holiness, and to experience the fullness of God's love and grace. His presence within you is a constant reminder that you are never alone; God Himself is with you, leading and strengthening you every step of the way.

The Role of the Holy Spirit in Understanding God's Word

The Holy Spirit plays a crucial role in helping you understand and apply God's Word. Jesus promised that the Holy Spirit would guide His followers into all truth (John 16:13), and this promise is fulfilled as the Spirit illuminates the Scriptures to you. Without the Holy Spirit, the Bible can seem like just another book, but with His guidance, the Word of God comes alive, revealing its depth, power, and relevance to your life.

The Holy Spirit acts as your teacher, opening your eyes to the truths in God's Word and giving you insight into its meaning and application. He helps you to understand complex passages, to see the connection between different scriptures, and to grasp the heart of God behind His commands. More than just head knowledge, the Holy Spirit enables you to internalize the Word, letting it shape your thoughts, attitudes, and actions.

As you read and study the Bible, the Holy Spirit brings clarity and conviction. He reveals areas of your life that need transformation, encourages you with God's promises, and empowers you to live out the principles of the Word. He also reminds you of what you have learned, bringing scriptures to your mind in times of need, whether for comfort, guidance, or to combat temptation. This ongoing interaction with the Holy Spirit makes your study of God's Word a dynamic and life-changing experience.

2. Empowerment for Witnessing

Power to Be Effective Witnesses

One of the primary purposes of the Holy Spirit's indwelling is to empower you to be a witness for Christ. Acts 1:8 declares, *"But ye shall receive power, after that the Holy Ghost is come upon you: and ye shall be witnesses unto me both in Jerusalem, and in all Judaea, and in Samaria, and unto the uttermost part of the earth."* This empowerment is not just for church leaders or evangelists; it is for every believer, enabling you to share the Gospel with boldness, clarity, and love.

The power of the Holy Spirit equips you to testify of Jesus, not just with words but through your life. He gives you the courage to speak about your faith, the wisdom to answer questions, and the discernment to know when and how to share. The Holy Spirit also works through you with signs, wonders, and miracles, confirming the message of the Gospel and drawing people to Christ.

Being an effective witness is not about your ability but about yielding to the Holy Spirit's power. As you rely on Him, He directs your conversations, opens doors for ministry, and prepares the hearts of those you speak to. The Holy Spirit also empowers you to live in a way that reflects Christ, making your life a powerful testimony of His love and grace. Your words and actions, empowered by the Spirit, can lead others to encounter the living God.

Living a Spirit-Led Life

Living a Spirit-led life means allowing the Holy Spirit to guide your decisions, actions, and responses. Galatians 5:16 encourages believers to *"walk in the Spirit, and ye shall not fulfil the lust of the flesh."* This instruction emphasizes that the Holy Spirit is not just a helper in times of need but a constant guide for everyday living. To live a Spirit-led life is to be in tune with His leading, sensitive to His promptings, and obedient to His voice.

The Holy Spirit's guidance covers every area of your life, from major decisions to everyday choices. He leads you in the paths of righteousness, directs you away from danger, and prompts you toward opportunities that align with God's will. As you cultivate a relationship with the Holy Spirit, you learn to recognize His voice and to distinguish it from your own thoughts or external influences.

Living a Spirit-led life also means bearing the fruit of the Spirit—love, joy, peace, patience, kindness, goodness, faithfulness, gentleness, and self-control (Galatians 5:22-23). These characteristics are evidence of His work in you, shaping your character to reflect Christ. As you yield to the Spirit, He produces these fruits in your life, impacting your relationships, your attitude, and your witness to the world.

To live a Spirit-led life, it's important to stay connected to the Holy Spirit through prayer, worship, and time in God's Word. Invite Him into your daily decisions, ask for His guidance, and be willing to follow wherever He leads. The more you depend on the Holy Spirit, the more you will experience His power, wisdom, and presence in every aspect of your life. This dynamic partnership with the Holy Spirit is what enables you to live fully as the new creation God has called you to be.

CHAPTER 9: WHAT TO DO WHEN...

1. Handling Wrong Thoughts

Recognizing Temptation and Escaping It

In your new life in Christ, you are not exempt from facing temptations and wrong thoughts. However, the Bible assures you that no temptation is beyond your ability to overcome with God's help. 1 Corinthians 10:13 states, *"There hath no temptation taken you but such as is common to man: but God is faithful, who will not suffer you to be tempted above that ye are able; but will with the temptation also make a way to escape, that ye may be able to bear it."* This verse underscores the reality that while temptations will come, God always provides a way out.

Temptation often begins with a thought—an idea, suggestion, or desire that opposes God's will.

Recognizing these wrong thoughts is the first step in overcoming temptation. It's important to be vigilant about what you allow into your mind, as your thoughts influence your actions. When you identify a thought that contradicts God's Word, you must take immediate action to reject it. This involves capturing the thought and bringing it into obedience to Christ (2 Corinthians 10:5).

God has equipped you with the tools to resist temptation. These include His Word, prayer, and the support of the Holy Spirit. When wrong thoughts arise, turn to Scripture for truth that counters the lie. Pray for strength and wisdom, and ask the Holy Spirit to help you discern the source of the temptation. Remember, you are not alone in your struggle; God is with you, providing the grace and power to overcome.

Remembering Your Identity in Christ

One of the most effective ways to handle wrong thoughts is to remember your identity in Christ. 1 Corinthians 2:16 says, *"For who hath known the mind of the Lord, that he may instruct him? But we have the mind of Christ."* As a believer, you have access to the mind of Christ, which means you can think as He thinks, align your thoughts with His, and reject anything that doesn't reflect His truth.

When you are tempted by wrong thoughts, remind yourself of who you are in Christ. You are a new creation, righteous, justified, and sanctified. You have been given a new mind, one that is not subject to the patterns of this world but is renewed by God's truth. This understanding empowers you to reject thoughts of fear, doubt, anger, or lust because they do not define you.

Whenever wrong thoughts try to invade your mind, declare your identity in Christ. Speak the truth of God's Word over yourself, affirming that you are a child of God, filled with His Spirit, and equipped to live in victory. The more you remind yourself of your identity, the stronger your defense against wrong thoughts will be. It's about training your mind to align with God's Word and standing firm in the truth of who you are.

2. Walking in Obedience

Embracing Justification and Reconciliation

Walking in obedience is a key aspect of living out your new life in Christ. This begins with embracing the truths of justification and reconciliation. Romans 5:1 states, *"Therefore being justified by faith, we have peace with God through our Lord Jesus Christ."* Justification means that you have been declared righteous before God, not because of your works but because of your faith in Christ. This gives you peace with God and the confidence to approach Him without fear or shame.

2 Corinthians 5:19 further explains, *"To wit, that God was in Christ, reconciling the world unto himself, not imputing their trespasses unto them; and hath committed unto us the word of reconciliation."* Through Christ, God has reconciled you to Himself, restoring the relationship that sin had broken. Embracing this reconciliation means accepting that you are fully accepted and loved by God. You no longer have to strive for His approval; you already have it through Christ.

Understanding your justification and reconciliation empowers you to walk in obedience. You obey not out of fear or obligation but out of love and gratitude for what God has done for you. Obedience becomes a response to the grace you have received, a way to honor God and align your life with His will. It's about living from your identity as a justified and reconciled child of God, not trying to earn a status you already have.

Practical Steps for Daily Victory

Walking in obedience and handling wrong thoughts require practical steps that you can implement in your daily life. Here are some steps to help you live in victory:

1. **Stay Rooted in God's Word:** Make it a habit to read, meditate on, and apply God's Word daily. The Bible is your guide for righteous living, providing wisdom, correction, and encouragement. When faced with challenges, let the Scripture be your anchor.

2. **Pray Continually:** Prayer is your lifeline to God, allowing you to communicate with Him, seek His guidance, and draw on His strength. Develop a consistent prayer life where you bring your concerns, temptations, and decisions before

God. Pray for discernment to recognize wrong thoughts and for the power to resist them.

3. **Renew Your Mind:** Continuously renew your mind by focusing on what is true, noble, right, pure, lovely, admirable, excellent, and praiseworthy (Philippians 4:8). Guard your thoughts by filtering them through the truth of God's Word. Replace negative or sinful thoughts with God's promises and truths.

4. **Surround Yourself with Support:** Connect with other believers who can encourage, support, and hold you accountable. Being part of a faith community helps you stay strong in your walk with God. Share your struggles and victories with others and allow them to speak into your life.

5. **Be Quick to Repent:** When you fall or make a mistake, be quick to repent and turn back to God. Acknowledge your errors, receive God's forgiveness, and move forward without lingering in guilt or condemnation. Remember, God's grace is sufficient, and His mercies are new every morning.

6. **Depend on the Holy Spirit:** Rely on the Holy Spirit to lead and empower you. He is your helper, guide, and source of strength. Ask Him to fill you daily, to give you wisdom in your decisions, and to empower you to live according to God's will.

7. **Declare Your Identity:** Regularly declare who you are in Christ. Speak God's promises over your life, affirm your righteousness in Him, and reject anything that contradicts His Word. Your declarations reinforce your faith and remind you of the victory that is already yours.

By incorporating these practical steps into your daily routine, you can walk in consistent victory over wrong thoughts and temptations. Remember that obedience is not about perfection but about a heart that is committed to following God. As you rely on His grace and take intentional steps to align your life with His Word, you will experience the fullness of your new life in Christ.

CONCLUSION

Summary of Key Points

As you have journeyed through the chapters of this book, you have explored the profound truths of your new life in Christ. From understanding your true identity as a spirit being created in the image of God, to embracing your transformation as a new creation, to recognizing the indwelling of the Holy Spirit, each chapter has been designed to build your faith and deepen your understanding of what it means to live in Christ.

You have learned that:

- **You Are a New Creation:** At the moment of your new birth, you were transformed into a brand-new creation. The old has passed away, and you are now a new person in Christ, filled with His righteousness and equipped to live a life that reflects His glory.

- **You Are a Partaker of God's Nature:** By receiving Christ, you have been given the nature of God. You are not just a follower of Christ; you are a child of God, with His Spirit dwelling within you, empowering you to live victoriously.

- **You Are the Righteousness of God:** Through Christ's sacrifice, you have been made righteous. This righteousness is not earned but given, allowing you to stand before God without guilt or condemnation, fully accepted and loved.

- **You Are Justified:** Your justification means that you have been declared not guilty. You are reconciled to God, at peace with Him, and free from the condemnation of your past. This justification empowers you to live confidently in your new identity.

- **You Are Sanctified:** God has set you apart for His purposes, sanctifying you through His Spirit. Your sanctification is both a one-time event and an ongoing process of becoming more like Christ, renewing your mind, and living a life that honors God.

- **You Are Delivered:** Through Christ, you have been delivered from the power of darkness and transferred into God's Kingdom. You are free from past bondages and equipped to live in the light of God's protection and grace.

- **God's Spirit Abides in You:** The Holy Spirit dwells within you, guiding, teaching, and empowering you to live a Spirit-led life. His presence is the guarantee of your inheritance in Christ and the source of your strength and wisdom.

- **What to Do When...:** In moments of temptation or challenge, you are equipped with the tools to overcome. By recognizing wrong thoughts, remembering your identity in Christ, and walking in obedience, you can live in daily victory.

Each of these truths is a cornerstone of your new life in Christ. Together, they form a solid foundation that empowers you to live boldly, joyfully, and purposefully as a child of God. This new life is not just about what you believe; it is about how you live, every day, in the light of your identity and inheritance in Christ.

Encouragement to Live Out Your New Life in Christ

Living out your new life in Christ is a journey, one that involves both learning and growing. It's about embracing your identity and living from the truth of who God says you are. There will be challenges along the way but remember that you are never alone. God's Spirit is within you, guiding you, strengthening you, and equipping you for every good work.

As you continue to walk with God, make it a priority to stay connected to Him through prayer, worship, and the study of His Word. Surround yourself with a community of believers who can encourage you, hold you accountable, and walk alongside you in your faith journey. Remember that growth takes time, and God is patient with you. He delights in every step you take toward Him, no matter how small it may seem.

When you face difficulties or when you fall, do not be discouraged. Remember that God's grace is sufficient for you, and His strength is made perfect in your weakness. Lean into His grace, rely on His Spirit, and keep moving forward. Your new life in Christ is not about striving for perfection; it's about pursuing a relationship with the One who has already made you perfect in His sight.

Let the truths you have learned in this book be a constant reminder of God's love, His power, and His purpose for your life. Live boldly as the new creation that you are. Embrace your righteousness, walk in your deliverance, and let the Holy Spirit lead you every day. As you do, you will experience the fullness of life that Jesus promised—a life that is abundant, purposeful, and gloriously aligned with God's will.

Final Blessing and Prayer for Understanding

As you close this book and step forward into your journey, may you be continually filled with the knowledge of God's love and the power of His Spirit. May the truths of your new life in Christ take deep root in your heart, guiding you, strengthening you, and empowering you to live in the fullness of His promises.

Prayer:

Heavenly Father, I thank You for each person who has journeyed through the pages of this book. I pray that the truths of their new life in Christ would be firmly established in their hearts. Open their eyes to see who they truly are in You, and give them the strength to live boldly as Your children.

Lord, may they walk in the confidence of their justification, the joy of their righteousness, and the freedom of their deliverance. Fill them with Your Spirit, guide them into all truth, and empower them to live lives that reflect Your glory.

I ask that You protect them from the lies of the enemy and from anything that would seek to pull them away from You. Surround them with Your peace, cover them with Your grace, and lead them on the path of Your perfect will.

Thank You, Father, for the incredible gift of new life in Christ. May each reader experience the depth of Your love and the greatness of Your power, now and always. In Jesus' name, Amen.

ABOUT THE AUTHOR

Nick Imoru is a dynamic speaker, author, educator, entrepreneur, and consultant based in Canada. He is the President of Achievers Centre, a division of Philips Reliability Consult Inc. Nick's mission is centered on empowering the human spirit through consulting, coaching, connecting and circulating ideas and information. His goal is to inspire, ignite passion, create profit, and make a spiritual impact, ultimately helping individuals bridge the gap between where they are and where they aspire to be.

Nick holds a B.Eng. in Mechanical and Production Engineering and an MSc. in Advanced Technology from the UK. With over 18 years of experience in the Oil and Gas industry, he specializes in Maintenance & Reliability Engineering and is a Certified Maintenance & Reliability Professional (CMRP), reflecting his commitment to excellence in his field.

As the author of over 15 books and numerous articles and research papers, Nick's work spans personal development, spirituality, academia, business, and finance. He is the founder of Achievers Consult, Achievers Centre, and Achievers Publishing, all operating under Philips Reliability Consult Inc.

Nick is happily married to Dr. Margaret and is a proud father of two daughters, Nelly and Myra. His unwavering dedication to personal and professional growth, combined with his entrepreneurial spirit, continues to make a profound impact on individuals and organizations, guiding them towards success and fulfillment.

With a vision to inspire, train, develop, and unlock potential, Nick Imoru is committed to helping individuals and businesses achieve their highest levels of success.

To contact Nick or learn more about Achievers Centre, opportunities, speeches, and seminars, please use the information below:

Email: Nick@achieverscentre.com
Website: www.achieverscentre.com

BOOKS BY SAME AUTHOR

- A Heart for God
- Operating God's Private Lines
- Growing In Life
- Money & Pleasure: Trap of Purpose
- Success Buttons for Life & Academic Excellence
- The Making of Greatness
- Your Best Year Ever
- Nothing Just Happens
- How Did I Become Like This
- Achievers Daily Tonic
- Living in His Fullness: Unveiling the Life, Mission, Death and Triumph of Jesus
- Your Belief System: How Your Thoughts Dictate Your Life
- The Wit & Wisdom of Dr David Oyedepo
- The Tongue: How Your Words Shape Your Destiny
- Kings Don't Beg, They Make Decrees

- He Has Said...So We May Boldly Say
- Character: The Blueprint for a Great Future
- Living in His Light: Understanding Your New Identity in Christ
- Personal & Family Budgeting: Mastering Your Money for Financial Freedom
- Your Money, Your Future: A Student's Guide to Financial Success
- Choosing the Right Path: A Career Guide for Teens and Youth
- The 21 Life Rules Every Child Should Live By
- Saving Your Future: A Practical Guide to Financial Literacy
- The Power of Your Environment: How Your Surroundings Shape Your Life
- Think It, Do It: How to Turn Thoughts into Meaningful Action
- Adventures in God's Amazing Storybook, Part 1
- Adventures in God's Amazing Storybook, Part 2

To order any of these books, please visit:

Our online shop @ www.achieverscentre.com

or any of the amazon websites:

www.amazon.ca or www.amazon.com or www.amazon.co.uk, etc

www.ingramcontent.com/pod-product-compliance
Lightning Source LLC
Chambersburg PA
CBHW050012040726
47599CB00014B/1339